Another Hunger
John Fennelly

smith|doorstop

Published 2018 by
Smith|Doorstop Books
The Poetry Business
Campo House
54 Campo Lane
Sheffield S1 2EG

Copyright © John Fennelly 2018
All Rights Reserved

ISBN 978-1-910367-85-8

Designed and Typeset by Tim Morris
Printed by Biddles Books

Smith|Doorstop Books are a member of Inpress:
www.inpressbooks.co.uk. Distributed by NBN International,
Airport Business Centre, 10 Thornbury Road, Plymouth, PL6 7PP

The Poetry Business gratefully acknowledges the support
of Arts Council England.

Supported by
ARTS COUNCIL
ENGLAND

Contents

7	Chaser
8	The Present
9	Altar Boys
11	A Lost Blue Peter Badge
12	Eucharist
13	Dad's Last Dog
14	Another Hunger, 1957
16	Letter Home
17	My Father's Glass Eye
19	Oscar And Lord Alfred
20	Ariadne
22	Westminster Bridge, 24th June 2016
23	Making Morning Flight
24	Road of Spoons
25	Pre-mortem
27	Another Hunger, 20th August 2013
28	Larkin in Paradise
29	Those Flowers
30	Last Night Nerves
31	Snow

To Mary and i.m. Bill

*...but if I could believe
That were a double hunger in my lips
For what is doubly brief.*

— 'The Two Kings', W B Yeats

Chaser

Mum sent me to fetch at least a score
before you frittered
all your wages in the pub or bookie,

and I found you in The Fellowship,
Sweet Afton smoke, navvy's boots,
neatly sculpting ruffs
round emptied pints of porter.

Holes, roads, tube lines
you dug and drank, I swore
you'd never see me travel.

Listening to the bodhrán
of rain over London, now I crawl
the craic through East End pubs,
Grave Maurice, Blind Beggar,
Hung, Drawn and Quart'ed,

still searching, with my map
of London's Lost Rivers,
draught and redrafts on my lips
an overdraft in my pocket.

But in yours, betting slips.
Crafty dead cert smiles.
And while I haunt these places
still alive, I find I'm more
of a gambling man, Dad,
than I bet you'd ever have guessed.

The Present

We had gone to the barn on Boxing Day
pushing the door on cow quiet and dark.
A shape swung in the winter we'd let in
and wee Evie ran towards him laughing,
tiptoeing to reach the soles of his shoes.

Uncle Sean really could do anything
and walking on air, this was a new game,
necktie face pulling, hanging from a beam.
Then she was silent like looking up
to a crucifix. Sucked her thumb. Sought my eyes

that hadn't seen him wear a suit before.
Even on Sundays. Now he would wear one
always, like Dad, when they laid him out
to wake and I was her age. Men standing
outside, black tied, *sorry for your trouble,*

which must have been to lose this choking stone
in my chest, kept steadfast, hard held promise
to make me a man you'd never see cry.
Hands, spat on for work, a clout or shaken deals,
lift ink-black pints that contract the tongue to silence.

Altar Boys
i. m. R C

I

In the must and candle smoke smell
of cotta on cassock, white over black over jeans,
we sped away from the requiem altar
in Father Murphy's Ford Cortina
to the cemetery and its ceremony, the grave.

Bird-pocked, still, angels stood, empty handed
looking skyward or intent on silent prayer
bent marble heads, inspecting deteriorations.
Like the inscriptions annotated by urban fox,
or décor, Inter-Flora, we thought little of permanence.

Then fists of earth thumped someone old we didn't know,
swinging the incense we called Holy Smoke,
glad to bunk off being buried alive at school,
finding you could swap Crystal Palace Cards,
conkers and sweets more easily at a funeral.

II

The route to the grave is more difficult now
you in this box twenty three years on,
my Red Bus Rover, Dick Whittington,
speaker of sand-play language, first day,
St. Augustine's: compacting grains to shapes in air.

III

At the source of the Ravensbourne one day
we found a skull and were so thrilled
we took it to the Museum, thinking *Dinosaur!*
Catching the bus up from Down,
we unearthed a Professor of Bones,

pallid palaeontologist at The Horniman,
who explained the 'Eynsford Otter', one hundred
years extinct, since it crossed the border,
paw width, between the stream and death.
Even though the past can not build a dam

so you can slow the waters, cross the Lethe
with slivers of tree and leaf, I still know
how we were and will be: altered, yet as we are.
Like love. Structures of bones and words
found by river banks, beyond the grave and that above.

A Lost Blue Peter Badge

Hours spent standing to
in a cold south London
pre-fab hut, watching Akela
and Brown Owl hog the three bar heater,
eat our crisps, before the game
of British Bull-dog.

It must have been their idea
to take us on that jamboree
where we undressed:
scarves slipping toggles,
badged jumpers pulled from sweaty static,
browned up as Native Americans.

All the arrows scattered
from my fairy liquid quiver, when we
were chased by the scouts in cowboy
hats, brandishing cap-guns,
volleys of cordite and naive racism,
hollering in the rain past the dignitaries.

Head dress, bow, shorts discarded,
I shivered and cried in the shower after
older boys drew back wet towels
to print V welts on legs and arse.
My flights, so carefully twined in ash,
left tangled in the shame and mud.

Eucharist

Thankful, though its cool, wild dark invited,
I played statue and would not run on
with the other children to the hide and seek woods,
all bramble, thorn, nettle and velvet moss.

Siobhan had told me how babies were made:
a powder from what boys have, that girls don't.
And with that, she slipped her hand in my pocket
to pinch my last Flying Saucer full of sherbet.

I would have been eleven, hot-cheek astonished,
in love with her skipping off laughing with my sweet,
who would soon, *fruit of thy womb*, magic babies.
It was Our Lady's Primary last summer visit

to the Isle of Wight and, from time to time, I think
I am still entranced there in the long grass
leading from the cliff top to the kiss-chase copse,
the rice paper melting on her tongue.

Dad's Last Dog

Troy sensed me first, arriving home
for the funeral, as him or his ghost
seeming to surface on the frosted front door glass.
Family resemblances, inhaled pheromones:
tobacco and whiskey, that he'd not associated
with the beeswax, embalming fluid, Brasso.
In the hall he was a wagging, paw splayed obeisance

and the heart he'd only known
as insistence, like smells, hunger, running,
was squeezed as in a vice to whines,
as if he were learning too late, old dog,
to play on it like an ocarina

when the key was turned and he realised for the last time
that I was not his master. He was not coming back.
Whimpered to his corner, would not even lift his head.
Stayed there moulting for about a week.

Another Hunger, 1957

> *Too much love drives a man insane,*
> *you broke my will*
> *oh what a thrill...*
>   Jerry Lee Lewis

Duck-arse combed. Brilliantined.
Armoured in boots and biker leathers,
astride a 'goes like a gun' Enfield,
with all the drastic measures

taken —smoothed pearls of regret—
a few memories like bullet wounds
that wouldn't heal.
On the deck my father sits

twisting the throttle. The moon's pull
on the dancing tide's ceíli hold,
muscle flex, wave fall,
swing embrace and release,

shakes the ferry in rattles and rolls
of wash and rush to the harbour wall.
Tumbling seas like rock-a-billy girls
all petticoat flounce, jive and swell.

Wishes. Steam off frothy coffees.
Taste. Kissed port 'n' lemon lips
singing along to Eddie, Gene, Elvis.
He'd not be first or last who escapes

from a past, kick started by songs,
revved on desires, young, fresh,
as if I know from where I get these pangs
and sure 't 'd be a great place, but for the English,

across the water, away from Our Fathers,
rebels without a clue or ghosts of a chance,
all that land and gun palaver,
the prying priests at every dance.

Letter Home

> *'The headed paper made for writing home*
> *(If home existed) letters of exile.'*
> Larkin, 'Friday Night in The Royal Station Hotel'

Last boat-train gone, double room rate too high,
checks-in any way to check out— bed, chairs
and en-suite. Life would choose differently.
Leaves the bar last when the bell declares
the mini-bar open to the dregs, glass
by glass. His last word left between them reads
as an old testament, how it came to pass,
as well end it here as Ireland or Leeds,
that abuse of love in The Colony Room.

The bath will have congealed cold red by dawn.
How the maid will scream. So, razor blade it is—
years in England of neither peace nor home
though work, sure, as blood fronds the water: now
his name's sighed in a few Laois villages.

My Father's Glass Eye

I

After seven operations failed
to reignite the real one, he came home with three,
two of polymethyl resins, lifelike
silk veins and iris indecisive blue
or green. His spare would stare
from the mantlepiece
so we'd always catch it,
his eye of providence.

Or later down the Irish Club
he'd place his Sunday Best
next to his stout,
I'm keeping my eye on you.

II

Lost navvying the Jubilee Line,
impaled on some thorn of steel
to a fascinating absence: glimpsed
satin behind a smooth curtain of skin
whenever he'd sleight it out or in.

Relishing this, especially on buses,
his motorbike sold. Index finger inserted,
he'd then pop it in his mouth
suck briefly its lozenge, give it a wipe
then deftly lift the tear thirsty flap
and pop it back.

At night, drink taken,
he'd often forget to take it out
and be found in the living room,
a snoring barrel of black,
iris enfolded back to read his dreams,
its white disc staring like the moon.

III

My lips on his cold forehead. Both eyes
finally closed. Undertaker's lies.

IV

I picture the green glass eye
is soon stilled to balance
on its cornea fulcrum
in the bowl of the skull
the pupil fixed
to scan the fathomless dark.
Above, the émigré trains flash past.

Oscar And Lord Alfred

An Irishman and an Englishman
walk into a bar, a hundred years hence,
one orders absinthe, the other creme de menthe,
and sit in the snug reserved for the avatars.

I've had a Brain Tweet © from the Pope,
congratulating me on my reincarnation,
and one from her wife, a commission,
the reincarnation of the green carnation.

The Englishman, younger, blonde, remains
silent, tense. *Let us kiss and so farewell,*
though to lose you twice might seem negligent,
I wanted you to know, sweet Bosie, there was nothing I could do.

Joyce has switched off Nora, Beckett forgone Suzanne,
Aosdána's adamant it hasn't the funds
to keep its writers' partners eternally on show.
And each man has to kill the thing he loves ...

Ariadne

Fucked and chucked, screwed then eschewed:
my footnote in myth, a minor Minotaur celebrity:
naive girl beguiled by tall, dark, handsome hero.

It's little wonder then that I found solace in Bacchus,
his constant liquid kisses, how he's up all night
pre-eminent—my god, and priapic.

Don't think my heart mended though
after that faithless piece of shit, all bull,
crept away while I slept

and I woke to search the bay of our embraces,
the whole Isle of Naxos
only to find absence, his boat

shrinking to a speck as my eyes filled.
I smile now for his father's bones that in such haste
he forgot to hoist the white sails. Promises. Promises.

No man saw my agony for the death
of my human hearted brother, the end of faith
and not just the loss of my brute lover

who I helped survive him with my thread snagging
back through that crafty maze
after the merciless, mercy killing.

I'd known since he'd been weaned and was biting,
then of a sudden hidden away, how he longed to be free
of the rage of his appetites

the bewildered guilt, the keening
mad loneliness of knowing what he was. His loyal sister
his only hope of escape from the charnel filth of that labyrinth

Westminster Bridge, 24th June, 2016

Us. Thames. On the night bus, stuck in traffic,
yawning office cleaners off to begin shifts;
amid these high rise hopes swim regrets
like fish in lost rivers, all *buts* and *ifs*.
Each stop is a glottal moan of *'kin' 'ell*.
Only *Human Capital*, just the plural, goods,
in these sleep-rise, repeat, headphone babels.

Estate agents trade postcodes, gangs deal 'hoods,
cranes, lit Ts, tap skies. Roofs, serrated knives,
where all the world stands and delivers
their cash, identity, dignity, then lives
to a bit of marsh round the bends of rivers.
Fascists snatch a bridge, smash it to a pier
given carte blanche, a green light, smelling fear.

Making Morning Flight

Will count down miles then try and get some kip
on the motorway's aquarium of flashing night,
a sequinned cascade of headlamp and brake light,
where I'm a pulse to my fingers, tongue, lips
in sodium bursts, cat's eyes, dashes of glare,
all transitory, making connections
strewn on hard shoulders, central reservations,
head pressed on its reflections: in here, out there,
welcome aboard this midnight bus to Luton,
in rain, now, that's all light smear and wipe,
with a bladder full of beer and 'In Use' sign on,
my thumbs peck at the screen's predictive type
to lullaby iambs in a sonnet's kiss goodnight
and dream Prague's golden spires, where I'll alight.

Road of Spoons
After watching Lanzmann's Shoah

There's a lake at the centre of Europe,
waters lapping shores of ash.

A disused train line, winter trees
and what were thought leaves, in black and white,

become, close-up, thousands of spoons
or tens of thousands, between tracks

that scrape to cold horizons. That oval
held by a mother, teased

her weaning child's mouth to a tunnel,
this, a last meal, or was lifted by bride

and groom to the other's lips
once at a wedding feast. Or these, handles

becoming menorahs or mirrors, sharper than knives.
At night each spoon's scratched whirl,

a miniature lake, gives back full
a sky's scarred bowl.

Pre-mortem
after Odysseus Elytis's 'The Autopsy'

And so I found on the sole of each foot
an A to Z of every London street,
and like the back of my hand
each tramline in Brno,
Kerry turf and Prague dust.

On each lobe, sensual as apricot,
and in the helix of each ear
a little salt to show the weather
must have been fierce,
on the seas over which my people came.

Listen. It's uncanny
how inside you can hear
wanderings on empty beaches, the oceans
and what loneliness sounds like there.
Lungs and liver remonstrate

I was not run over by a bus tomorrow.
And the bruising around the mouth?
A rare result of every kiss
coming as one hell of a smack
as others' lives are said to flash before them.

The flame that still burns above the pubis
is a phenomenon often noticed
on those who left, or were left
before desire ceased,
extinguished to no great or greater loss.

Even this stinking abscess
of cancerous bile: words unsaid that should have been,
words said that shouldn't
in the cavity of the unreturned book and smile,
it's not that either that did for me,

but the way I found each incision
was the cry of a different animal in the night,
how the moon had disguised itself behind my eyes
the clouds floating in the stilled retina, the flecks in the iris
gathering to a murmuration of regret.

Another Hunger, 30th August, 2013

Then there I was, a weeping head
pressed against the architrave
on hearing he'd died that day.

Not one gassed child in Syria
had induced a tear,
but he, my lachrymator

and there were many more
than one for every year.
Just another bloody gasman.

But I am afraid. Very afraid,
knowing a boy somewhere
will wrap around a bomb

to make the dead air
a moment's blizzard of blood and bone
or a girl point blank in the head, going to school,

that the loving as the unloved
have nothing to lose.
That poetry makes nothing happen

but to mind the tongue, éist the mouth
for a voice of glacier melt and scree.
Only turf grass bows to the wind,

and in the rain pelting the Brough,
blade and leaf flicker with each drop
as night gathers to drench us.

Larkin in Paradise

Superb jazz library. Glenlivet Rivers.
And though fascism and onanism
are explicitly frowned upon, especially by women,
who still give me the shivers,
it's difficult to break old habits in the afterlife.

So once I am sure not much is going on
I can't resist the crisp cellophane
I slip a fresh spank mag from.
Hard to explain how much infinity is tedium
and there's an awful lot more of it to come.

Heaven is a lot like Hull.
Boats come and go
and angels squabble
over trumpets
like bitchy sea gulls.

Those Flowers

I

I caught him yesterday, my younger self,
drinking Guinness, reading a book.
He followed me, hang dog
to at least two other pubs
before I had the nerve to ask
What the fuck is going on?
He tried that 'old man I know thee not'
but I saw right through him,
the sanctimonious, love-sick little shit.
You'll end up like me, I kept shouting
in my distress, till the police were called
and I was half-nelsoned into the ambulance.

II

This fella, who looked like my dad,
lost it in the pub last night.
He'd bought me a pint
seemed all right. Picking
up my copy of Heaney, he turned.
Said he still loved me
and how little time there was,
but I'd be his forever, how he could
never leave me. When he started shouting
Never send those flowers
in my face, fists clenched
on my lapels, *or you'll end up like me!*
It was then the barman called the police
who arrived with the ambulance.

Last Night Nerves

All the world's a stage and most of us are desperately unrehearsed.
   Sean O'Casey

Cold glow pooled Down Stage Centre.
The moon follow spots like a skulking spy
of the times behind trees or city backdrop
watching stories played out as tragedy then farce
to an empty house where makeshift others
whose auditions to be me they almost passed,
stand in wings and stage whisper *sincerely luvvy?*

Or suddenly I'm the provincial Doctor, in love for years,
secretly, pretending there's nothing to forgive,
seeming to play idly with a gun in Act II. Curtain.
No wonder some prefer to watch a dog bait a bear
and chances are tomorrow we won't be here
we'll go dark, no bums on seats, melted to air.
Let's talk about it on our death bed, sweetie, our wings

stuffed in pillows now the angels won't invest
and air kiss at the fall of the final curtain.
Then staff broken, my Shakespearian ear worm
and I will bow O! Ow! Out of the fizz of limelight
the end of the run, the house lights up,
the whole globe a mote of floating dust.
Notes: *this isn't a dress rehearsal, darling.*

I'm closing this whole damned show the way it opened—
naked—with the panic peristalsis of the bulb and mirror
eating act, blow torched nerves in final stage fright
at the not fake blood in the toilet bowl
or crystal rainbow pixels of a full body scan
screen tests, biopsies and specimens
of all that I am.

Snow

Furred rain, turned down to silence, layers soft
flurries down light flues in thrilling cold spells
of ice bling, jacked from the dark and flung as frost
for arms and legs to crick and print to angels.

Improbable manna of distant stars
dance, unique as loves or lives. What were the odds?
Gravity in time does for them on streets, parks, cars—
that blank to the stares of poker faced gods

at our numb fingered panic, which is just
to hi-five time aloft like nudged balloons—
for avalanche has to, as black ice must.
Like sleet on tongues our thousand or so moons,

the skid, the smothering, even this sonnet
a page turned to white, silent, infinite.

Acknowledgements

Thanks to Bare Fiction for commending 'Eucharist' in 2016.

Thanks to all at Smith|Doorstop for their hard work. To Carol Ann Duffy for believing in me. My gratitude to Michael Symmons Roberts for his invaluable guidance. Thanks also to Mark Pajak, Zaffar Kunial and Helen Mort for their support, insight and great conversation. To Dan Gretton and Gareth Evans for nurturing the initial impulse and all my friends and family for their love and support.